ROBERT BRIDGE

A MIRRORED WOMAN

To   Vivien

Watch me go... . enjoy !!

02 07.07 R.B.

Br@ndBook
London Publishing

Title: A MIRRORED WOMAN

© Copyright Robert Bridge
© Copyright **Br@ndBook London Publishing**

First edition 2006

Project of the cover: Francesco Bernardini
Edited by Marzena Majewska

Typeset by
Michał Gramatowski

Printed by
Pod Gryfem – Hieronim Osowski – Poland

Published in the United Kingdom by
Br@ndBook London Publishing

ISBN 0-9553162-5-1

e-mail: bookshop@brandbook.co.uk

www.brandbook.co.uk

A MIRRORED WOMAN

ALL WOMAN

All woman
with hips sloping as a convection
tight enough to bare children
and when you wear jeans you do
the pockets justice
just as the zips or buttons may
resemble Brazilian slips
that would double up and puff out majestically
mini skirts would certainly do no justice
yet pink suits you like a camouflage back pattern
disguising your doughy strength
which you keep packaged like a parachute
if you open up your assets
I'd hit the ground with full force
only lips which keep my eyes flashing
glossing over teeth fully grown
and San Francisco city buildings
whiter than your brassiere
I guess
When you lick your lips
with mouth still ajar
my attention becomes drawn to those
blue lapis lazuli gems and the dilation's
that furthers my attention to your beauty
perfection would be an understatement
But the flip flops show your size 5
an the nails shine like girders
which do your hair and skin-tone justice
look into MY eyes and read you infantry

THE TONGUE OF FIRE

Speaks almost snake like...
    Venomous Maori welcome
Let's frame the features with a necklace of petals,
Multi coloured,
Welcome to the flap of unsolicited flesh that's as sensitive,
Sensitive as the paste that keeps the dragon breath at bay,
You lick your teeth after late nights of Indian restaurants,
The coriander seems only trapped well fresh,
And on the motor way,
    Oh the temptation to lick of the moisture,
Instead you flick on the heater,
I felt my tongue melt from the supermarket window,
Whilst you, you, you...
Words can not describe the intimidation of you waving your
Tongue on passing my yard in your Skoda,
I know you, I know your financial stability,
    I also know all about perversions
Or I can guess,
    When it turns, turns, turns the tongue of fire,
    Burns, burns, burns the flames a higher,
Welcome to the local drive by,
    You best just drive on,
    Cause the flap of your tongue press buttons.

IKEA WOMAN

Tell me mighty pageant of Ikea
    (As I flip through your pages)
If I emboss crayons upon your already inscriptions
    (Already well thumbed chapters)
Or defy my goblins of indifference to differ price ranges
    (Digging in the dust of scanty conjectures)
Though your fervent zeal shines on the moon
And your chair of Sweden fly fit for a Northern Princess
    (Mulberry the perfect choice for a cross section)
And the pages pillaged applying my own Feng Shui
Like an ancient Pall Mall magazine cover deceiving yet
    (Fitting voor de younger)
Leaping lady's Sky clad like a red light district
    (Being sure to rotate regularly)
Knowing the boundaries of dimension
Allowing the small change to frogger across a lampshade
Being sure to pull those bursting buds of Venetian
    atmospheric changes
Surely be it a privilege to scavenge and adapt
The picture you once faked yourself
Or just to hand it appropriately as a crucifixion

PIE MOCHA

From the Bastille of a Basted jacket
Or the hand that feeds from a bucket
When you chew this pie from Ken tuck it
You generally learn how to suck it
After you have moped all of the seeds
That reminisce apples left on wasted walks
Only this parish seems forlorn in participation
or those bells of Kentucky ring like an infection
of a sweet tooth
Mama tell the truth
You filled this pie with a tenement and a whistle
Mama laughs through here stuffing's of the edge
of a bristle
With a cream moustache
And your nose cries pistachio
The recipe equates chopped up oak and a cinnamon

OPITO DE NEIUVE (SNOWFLAKE)

Towards the Chinese bamboo sugar can gates
Bonsai branches, taboo, hoi pain awaits,
Pet rescued through the armada of extradition.

Unusual bleaching of sunglasses needed
Gorilla's a screeching for the malt molasses that bled
Skin tone reproduced one in ten thousand.

Tears burn cheeks like skin cancer increasing
Molecular cells peak might win white blood winning
Herbal remedy, Calamity try and fail.

Preying beyond the laughing Buddha,
Snowflake siesta, hasta la-vista,
Curling cure finger white over red retina

Snowflake in season its never to late,
Yet if Snowflake is leaving this volcanic quake,
Swing to the next branch and fight the cancerous
Michelin.

BLOKES

Back patio or else we will eat upon the lawn
Just like when you were first born,
Spoilt from birth like mothers cooking,
How you began peeling apple cores,
Sultana apple's stuffing chores,
Bores, bores waiting religiously for brown sugar,
To mess up another perfectly average childhood.

WHY ARE YOU FIXING ON FEELINGS?

You and that caravan
Your assistant knows you're the man
An your insistent precautionary measures
Volunteered to dish out addicts paraphernalia their treasures
An swabs upon thumb tips to prevent bruising
All around town addicts you were cruising
Pine disinfectant and vials of citrus
And warnings on that poster of the piercing of the clitoris
That's why sedation and method were the only means
Eventually knows addicts could be weaned
And years hence still on distribution
Your front line views were a valuable contribution
I valued your views on addiction
But I noted your mind and its colossal infliction
Yours feelings were not timid nor neither in grace
But the lines of frustration were just written upon that face
The wait of it all levied from that smile
Only the crease of your smile
Seemed inviting during acting out
But now that I'm clean and smoothed out the grout
I could take your infantry I class you as a friend
Feelings for feelings could make as an am mend
Of the help you provided an the dedication
To this fear
Of loosing the battle
Or to just beating the bear

INTERVIEWING THE CLEANERS

Open up the outskirts of iniquity
      close the gate then enter
Walk through the Tishamarsh garden
      observe the Rhododendrons
Step carefully on our pathway
      love pleasant surprises
An on the name of the estate press
      that button disguised as oh
Observe how eggshell paint and
      perfectly polished windows
Silhouette your reflections
      as I keep up waiting
Look beyond your reflection and
      observe personal hygiene cleaners
From an agency £15 hourly
      to the agency
Ring again your patience may well do you favours
      ring a third time an the melody rings jingle bells
Enter an estate you may never see the likes again
      poetry paid for most things
Where theirs a will there's a way
      Ushered from the corridor to the cloakroom
I may check your pockets
      for crumbs leaflets receipts
Hand your coat upon the diplodocus spinal column
      dinosaurs gave me so much inspiration
Observe the room whilst I boil
      the kettle one lump I guess
You taste the brew immediately out of politeness
      I'm proud of your tolerance to lip service
Flicking through the scenic patterns of a carpet look up man I need
      your motivation we may one day be friends
Imagine earning more money than the rest of your life say

12

£25 an hour
    if your good now's your chance to appeal
You speak simple and say the bare minimum I can't figure
    you out can you not see me scratching my chin
Your appreciation of those dazzling Chandeliers
    adjures to my approval
But will you fetch my slippers
    So I ask you a question
I know you're a bullshitter but what can I say
    You are perfect

BEDTIME

This pillow is puffy
it will help you sleep
The water bottle
will warm your feet
Today WAS a hard day
so get your rest
If you like I can strap on
your favourite vest
I know that this night
 is all queasy
An I love when you dose
well that pleases me
Your bath I guess was squashy
yes wishy washy
Which will encourage
great dreams
I will always be with you
 to comfort the themes

And the stories of shining armour protect you
Or the never land fables shall map out this night
    Sleep
        Sleep
            SLEEP (whispered)
                You know you just might
                    Goodnight

TRAP DOOR

As I opened the door an trapped a finger
I screamed a compulsive discontent
As a musty smell of a crucifying linger
She could tell I was *cross* and hell-bent
As she gave me that cold tap
And gagged me with a plaster
I realized that pain was crap
And that all I was was faster
Than the last time the doors were opened
I felt slightly more chilled
But this frightful night I hoped
Would soon become distilled
Like a beaker of holy water
That is malted stored then milled
Into my deep sub-conscious
Sounded better that a scream
I guess before this I was angry
She knew this all the same
So when this tomfoolery
Happened it was only I to blame

BULET POINTS

The present time of entering a question about what
    Bullet points
You questioned I answered for what seemed like an hour
    Many valuable points
I knew where it would end but not when it would stop
    I needed cold shower
The flowers were left on your office table a token of my power
    An the greeting said Dank ash urn
You had stemmed me down to many times and left me in crystals
    Food for the flowers
And you wonder why the lone sharks flocked my parameters
    Like a duck to water
I dived into this project and it cramped up my sides
    Like a lamb to the slaughter
Follow the rules follow the guidelines all put a-side
    And then guess what I bought her
One them new battery powered pencil sharpeners with a vice
    My pencil's were all blunt
Well I guessed if I though it would be nice
    And the bullet points
Seemed accurate and somewhat cleverly etched and traced
    With a pencil I presume
I thanked her for the bullet points and the way she cut the main
    For it's the basic re quest's that always
Kept us sain

PAPER HAIR

I am upset when I think of all the pain I have caused you
I am happy that you are in control
You are something I should strive for
So I put you on my to do list (as if I needed to)
One of these days we will look back and laugh
If not but for the life we were not to live
Then the life surely could be different today
but this is not about life (or death)
This is about progression
HAPPINESS
and human nature
When you first asked me to remove paper from your hair
On the way to get guitar and machine
I have been at your side of honour
Like the girlfriend I'd only dreamt of
And the feet felt levitation
Or several persona's (seven streams of consciousness)
Taken with a pinch of seaweed sea salt
With more than love or precision
If I were a cat you'd clear my mess
If only we were cats on the streets of P.C dibbles beat
You showed me the ways of Kleeneeze
An cooked a pepper as I requested
whilst the Dr kept us in during Saturday
Bar the seven streams of consciousness
(o.k. its only down the road)
I enjoy these patterns but your not just another poem
Nor cherub's injured bottom
Nor goddess of Adding ton's highest view point
You bigger and stronger than before
3 years of changing Mr men plasters
And downloading winyip

The tools of provision that was laid out in a bucket
that just sits out this very room
Has never gone to waste
(although the miracle glass cleaner is almost empty)
Everything just seems better
Your with me you always will
(there's so much I want you to see)
I want to wave my magic wand and break a debt or Bill
But you know my limitations
(that numbing down is such a thrill)
Let me nibble your nails as I always say
For your tomatoes are lucky bunch
So when your ready drop me a vine

BOX OF SECRTES

Birthday box wrapped in silk
with a rose stroop extract
mixed with milk
diluted finely with minimum amounts
for when you open the box
there's more boxes that accounts
to nothing

So you open the gold box only to reveal the silver
drinking your milk shake that pleases your lips
as the milk stalactites down on to your Cleavage
you blot this away and crush the mistake
then continue to open being sure not to break
the box made of ache

So you open the Oak box with chisel and hammer
continently lent from the guy down the Manor
only to find a box so small that it's made of bone
could this inside contain some intrinsic stone

So you open the bone box with a scalpel and mini mirror
hoping inside would make you eyes glimmer
though paranoid about what's in side
you continue on and watch the ride
your birthday was a belter
you spent all day opening presents

Well it's the thought that counted

THANKS FOR THAT DISSEMINATION

I read and read some till these eyes overflowed into
                                        symmetrical sauce
But the only common similarity found could well been that of
                                        desperation
For to write I needed to read and for this prophesy of good
                                        literature
Would need more than just elementary deductions with a tabac
                                        aromasaic
Not even the sculpture in the lemongrass would every confer
                                        the conifers
With a texture that seems to stir any free flowing mans Masonic
                                        degree
The day women stormed the position was the day I started this
                                        investigation
An my findings although ushered and undertaken followed some
                                        correlation
And leasing down from thou cobble stoned enivilation of
                                        experience
I knew the answer would progress again and again hence the
                                        subject
For I knew I'd find my prose in you like a faulty shadow
                                        repaired amplified

Rob B window this is your life

Starting on in poetry as a private
sharing all your struggle and strife

then moved on to be a published cell
to a harvested Anthology
television characters observed in that spell

but then you moved to Holland wrote poems on boat
never really got far or even left the Kade
observed three dimensional experiences stagnant, afloat

you never gave up not even through deportation
only to be offered to join Diabolo as an English editor
that was before you left Hoorne station, Stationery

what a boost from Dr Stewart and his motto
Light on from down the Manor upon a Napkin
Stewart said do it and since then I performed the Don

like a life that now seemed focused living emends
of open mikes and library mags
the days just flew the past with it blends

and the future's bright the poets stand strong
no one ever told you if you were wrong
you reached and typed a poem
you learned it recited words it just keeps on flowing
through poetry RobBWindow you learned to start
Growing

NAILED TO A COMPARISON OF COMPATIBILITY

She was an accurate scale of procession
With nails that curved like talons on progression
and the files and focus kept me guessing
She was more beautiful than a mouth full of nails
that I'd chewed and nibbled for days after
I could feel the depletion the witch grafter
Everything seemed flicked out the window
blocking the gut like a drainpipe requiring scaffolding
with a view of the comparison of nature
What with the North and the South
long and creased or short and shiny
always well polished with a brass knob for a reflector
I could see that the hands
nor the lines of palmistry could have predicted
the price of a nail job with added sequin's
I tried to help her but if I can't help myself
I just nibbled away like a corn on the cob
but I still saw her reflection in the brass knob
and the lines were somewhat of an open book
She was a genius when she cooked
so she banned me from the kitchen
Nailed a sign on the door give away no entry dead end
I moist end nails in hand cream and coco-nuts
in a particular blend
that would have ironed out those creases
If just her cat would not climb curtains
or scratch my best clothes
She just nibbled my feet and scratched my nose
So if I'm not welcome then what's the point
or the clippings of toenails all over the joint
All to be washed physique'ly cleaned vacuumed up
into a bag and emptied into the rubbish

Where it sat until some compromise or
secret handshake-like waiting for another nail to brake
and in this quake
I just kept loving her more and more
Galacticus would've been proud
Me and... Could save this planet with are nails alone.

FAIRY BIOPSY

Never the known Noni juice
drank from a shell of dreams
shell of suggestive sentinel soap scrub
healing the inside of man
The inside job of an outside injury
An the mystery awaiting the man
in a female land
domineered by consciousness

On a dark dream of waking up
in affirmations of
yesterdays injury
To only wake in
a stitched up wound
stitched in
faery dust
Little did a man know
about the honourable
memory of leaving
that tooth under the pillow

For days before as indeed
weeks after children
small folk smiled alike
The smile painted more
than just spiritual openings
Hello Fairies hello little people
he'd say on passing
the bridge
Fifty miles an hour
slowing down
in honour of his
imaginary Friends

24

The fairies could
do a fair old job on kings
But not one King would
ever be loved by just one
Faery

DRINK UP
DRUNK

I breathed your presence
and became drunk

That day booze, ever odeing
melted cocktail throat feather
Seemed to rush the lungs warm
leaving the skin the shade of leprassy

The bell a talisman a day of exuberance
ostricised for being powered by that fuel
the liquor
You thought that I didn't care
never noticed

But the truth was that
the bottle was ¾ qtrs full

If you could receive this intoxication
maybe attraction could become
diluted with bubbles

like cartoon thinking

FORGETFUL (NESS)

Notice the noticing words
T'was when that slip blurs
T'what was your name again
Noticing how always ends here
Five minutes of seriousness
Ends in the same silence
Every association upped sticks
For that one deviant brain
Sometimes short circuits
Leaving that path of separation
Leaving us separately
But how can I ever forget
The forgotten five minutes
Y'all in a name

FORGOTTEN (CELL)

Earlier today the happiness began
today is all a man needs

Far cry from yesterday's
metropolitan values

The freedom of sociable offerings
fallible and flimsy gone by

Experience enough for a clear
encapsulation chain

How the imagination fomentation
brewed pieces of bread

Medication only offer words
solidity of solitude merit

Batteries cost a week's wage
a price to pay for guilt

Tenacious external pattern
repeated with reference

HINGS GOIN'ON

Lady waiting for the four letter scruple of love
Over here right under those sexy eyes that
stare jukebox jaunty
Vulnerable and suggestive as me
you with the patent side
Enter a new world of moulding
inspiration new vision

Dance here in this breath
on fresh wind
the showers reservations
And together the spun out
emotional boundaries
politically distill
Never have a feeling such as this
crossed on so many vacations
I can never appose
the successful pleasure
shared on ice or tip

Ever

CHIAKUS-PLASTIC BOTTOM

Suddenly life goes
Forward whilst kissing stone cold
Heaven knows why ass

SWISH AND SWASH OF WAGES DAY

Swob the decks with fish water
Store the cattle in soiled salutations
Beef jerky before dry deckage
A packful of napkin sleepidge
Overcrowded pay-point
Tears donate freedom
Mans big wedge
A pretty medal
Sediment an
Alkaline

DISTANCE YOURSELF FROM THE BATTLE

The distance it seems is not only a social platter
But a political dish best ordered post renaissance
Matter of latency; honouring losses
Blatant breath of regimental copper soldiers
In a field of ethereal dust
In a glimpse it seems poetic
Nanoseconds nullified in pre-technology
Galleons diving like penguins
Sacrificial fathers of pawn
Led by confident leaders

WOE BETIDE: THE WRECKAGE

Navigation, Leadership, Foibles of Fluency

The sails send man to war
Wanted by the depths
The dungeon: Society

Bowling begins a bandwagon
And a whole new kettle of fish
The sieve caller: Bonaparte

Fresh as an ore
Oblong, symmetrical oracle
Black eyed telescope

INVARIABLE FURIOUS ANGER

And that's the reason why with furious angrer; my friend
would have stroked down upon that poor innocent fidget
He called it 'that no down, say means
nothing waste of a bar stool'

Anger Management: I used to quiz him, and he'd reply
'They never can get the numbers'
But really what he meant as I found out later on that evening
'She said paint your favourite Island
with everything you need'
Now there was also a mention of more females than males
Isolated disassociation
Sex: M/F
Violent thoughts/violent actions
Sex: A lack off

I guess when I saw the CD
with his ex lover on the front cover
Well we digressed and he continued...
'And she came right up to my nose and said'
'you're a very angry chap' in a high pitched east end accent

If I was funny there in that pub hearing the reaction
and in detail description of everything he required on his
deserted Island
but could not help feeling sad for the
manifestation of anger or the desolation
ideal islands
I felt tempted to tell him that: no man is an inland

But he'd already moved on to Aikido moves
he'd learnt two years ago

34

I just laughed shared back with him
I seldom get angry these days
Why you may ask
Cause am to bloody honest

ENVYISM

For in favouring you had it all singled out
Conglomerates buddies truckers horn and puffed pouts
Mesopotamian free and single
Those were the days when men left celibates
To there own devices
Sauna's cereal herbivores
Chomping battle uniform
Literate splices
Ready to expect the future for whom he's meant to be
Greek Goddess wrapped in hieroglyphic gantry
Eros arrow fired in a confusion of Psychometry
And pate on a platter with sex as a side salad

Education the physical means of persuasion
The family influence the homework invasion
With failure and signet stamped red wax upon its seal
Incense smell of lily's lime and Lagos
Polytheism any ism swash and swish of Pathos
With goose feathers fowling fluency
Falling feathers; the borrowing of apples
Mountain Everest near Mayan rope grapples
And being crook-shanked of stage
Arduous and envious of Man woman Land Mark
History Economics fellow triumphs
The tree's bark and politics
Punctuality and prohibition

ENVY

Those looks that said a korn of truth
That travels with us into recluse
Shying away from making quota's
Regretting the choice of pricing motors
The sympathetic pattern of admiring styles
Stagnating snippet's of dying smiles
And resenting the chemist's female hair dye
That only seep the sockets either way
so why is it that
When this reason wrapped in envy
Clouds the just for men see
Plastic gloves protect the potion
And feminine moisturizers slippy motion
Still leaves a face of coconut
Lotions wasted on lack of hair
Motors parked without care
Never receiving any particular ticket
This notion envious as seemingly stained
Still exists it still remains
Those frilly Swanettes *Men in tights*
Them ladders climbed
laddered sights
Disillusioned drama queen
Keeping all them windows clean

PERMIT ME TO INTRODUCE MY PRIDE

My pride
       Dammit When you said let go
       I was sure as hell you would not let it lie
       so lets go

       I'd been a man all those days and it stood me well
       hell I'd walked with millions, no mountains
       masquerading as the bread winner from them
throe's

       The buts and whens of falsified destiny
       The rest of me knew I was right and you were
wrong
       but the rest of your whispers echoed when

       I am a man these trainers have always indicated
       Vindicated my awareness at night on the street –
walk
       jogging with anyone remotely classed as family

       All this love and this pent up rage
       made me the ignorant passage
       like a vessel I'd moored then tried

       My thoughts of goodness trouble
       bubble wrapped in fashion and conformation
       You asked I answered but never truly felt it
Till now…

A WORTH WHILE RITUAL

Seven days of accumulating wax and rubbish
Not doubting the hexademical notation ching-gish
Vials of Royal jelly and Dragon root
Bathed in mouldy bags strained Orris Root
Focusing on visualizing Red and Black pentacle
Flame as a back drop of red and white household candles
Visualising the whole ecliptic season passed through daily
Routine
Hygiene psychically bathed in sanitation's of Acba
Web of protection acknowledging of past damage

Seven clear days of jotting down the feelings
Not something to be trifled with nor depromoted
A mixture of man and Goddess noted Neolithic rites
Favourite Neolithic sites of South
Protected by the watchtower (the old water pump)
Window watches patiently
As the breath of Shango follows...
Never look back
Tomorrow afternoon at noon this dissertation
Ritual of nature
Continues through the night in dreams
Of frolicking clockwise

Seven tree's mark out the circumference
One big branch with the horns splitting shape
To etch the sphere
Bubble Watched by quartets of elemental
Watchful dogs of the glen
Each tree nested a sugar free lemon throat fizzler
The immaturity of new age arguments
Do not govern this bubble
Pan and the spirit of the white cloth

Traded in and swapped for mere biodegradable uniform
Triple Goddess Cerridwen and the breast of chicken
I never do this calling on an empty stomach
The tree's act as a smoke screen
The sky a back drop
Manifestation of Gods in clouds
With the hammer of Thor and
the Elder Fulhark stammer
Not even the spirit of Christ misses invitation
Dream world for the faint hearted
Spirit of Broessoui
Man of more

Seven Golden spin offs like the flick of a coin
The currency of Chaos and the flap of wind rustled
Wishing away the well of Goblins and
Goblets of resuscitation
Following the old ways making them new
Acknowledging the failure of historical quotas
The flushing of the tides
The bin collection and seeing
Believing then communicating
True continuity and real love
Romantic primer of realistic faiths and expansion
Gradients of anomaly
Heredity of nature and owning it

WHITE FRILLS

Foucault fancy
Flint-ed legacy
Festive head-rest

THE GENRE NOTION

Drama came but the genre changed
As the story acted out
The antiquity almost rearranged
From an authors' point or view

Projection of the actors' elocution
On the pedestal's and stage
Travelled in a screeching electrocution
In the pentameter's of wage

Course and crevasse
Kong and crew
Worked the mighty Genre
With make up mad and bright
All the crew chipped in
Regardless of time of night

The cameramen were credit ted
As were the leading actors
The make up guys too
But the foundations of the contractors
Who designed the bloody set
They'd forgot to mention
The contract moist and wet

I thank you all directors
I thank you King and Queen
I thank you for a picture
Of me an this big screen
I also thank the watchers
At home on DVD
Or all the repeats on TV

And the interviews of me
Cause the genre
Was a fleeting fancy
We all shared about on set
It's only the extra bit
On DVD
That made this film it's premise

CONCERTINED POPPIES

One day, near time, with one shake, limp wrist action
Holder of English offerings wakes, and waits the folder fraction
The folds increase with plastic camouflage of black plastic
Almost conical, true red tape upon plastic carding
Dichotomy of what was left after war, wilted flowers
Survivors of Psycho-somatic heroism and faith of old leaders
(with a little help from skint necromancers)
Scarlett women hailed her handbag
upon many years of loose change
Paying for poppies, picture postcards, creased and symbolic
The sap of shear intervention, like speeches of silence
That congregate or crease, pinnered to the lapel
With no true intention of time, nor place
For many minutes that exist on the plains of truth
Inter folds and disguise life's true connotations
The spirit of wilting paper
Represents more than just a collection of memories
At the heart of plastic pondering (old ways)
Nor nanoseconds like; pellets of literate
Tablets of obituary

BIKE SHED

Meet me outside the bike sheds
With all your locks and chains
Release it in the flower beds
Got stuck between our brains

Air our lives in symthony's
Of which we shall not forget
Pop under you vectered limbs
Of you-to win-to bet

Will crawl beyond the bike sheds
Beyond the teams balloon
And crawl amongst grass threads
Skip to the baby boom

You treat me like you'd Hopscotch
your count and skip and scream
But you know this knee rocks
This mud is ours-our steam

We secretly met at a games world
We stood-we stuck-in mud
But you dangled on an twirled
Below my sack of spuds

LINTEL EYES

They stared upon the Woden fret work
Admired its contours, the streamed
Strong shoulder-she admired the twitch
keel cornered and starboard stare.

Then they exchanged thoughts...
As each abstract edge frailty
Sent vibrant notes nobbling;
Constantly observing her nose.

But if they ever imagined makers
Braking the news to the chair-maker
Because they'd «dream»t in an eye
Below the beautiful broken chair.

They stared upon this Nordic passage
Un-be-known to the repetitsious creator
Sent signals out by word of mouth;
Kitchen wrapped in chinese cloth.

MANX BUTCHER

Blood dried bench marks sprayed blue
Neutralising and Spock's vessels ahead
Press up inside the forehead of you
Waiting to put another lamb to bed.

Green vessels squirt stomach acid;
Detrimental to cloth, trapped rollers
Intestinal fingers crush bones placid
Hung around and trapped hour bowlers.

Salted skin floats to crystal hiding
Cut handles heavy and skinny rips
Trapped in the lairages residence
Hot wash so powerful it whips.

Electric volts; the edge of steel,
Quickly sharpens to frequent point
As flesh hangs for a weeks meal
Packaged; cryvacked an empty joint

HYPOCRISY

Something possessed by more than just an illusion
Clearer than any previous conditioning
With that freedom of genetic nurturing gave
The tie and suit, the polished black boots
Were never realised by any minister
He never judged me and I never judged him
So this be all true and well but that possession
Juxtaposed a hypocritical fantasy
Because every material time ticking Star Wars watch
Gave me affirmations of something more than
Astrological gazing, peeping into the window
Of next door neighbours Gazebo; plastic figures
Disassembled and revealed mother nature, Bandia,
Buddy L trucks; Lego legislation's all mindless
Rituals. Sometimes we'd all throw red berries
Poisoned by the days longing of soda
As apposed to the godly fruit of oranges.
Today it still seems like mixed messages
But one things for sure education reveals
The true heretics of Atheism, conforming
To the linguistic will of previous prodigies
Buried deep in literature and memory
With the funeral attended with more
Than just family, friends, worst enemies
simple humans waiting to feel the fuse
The switch clicking fingers to the rhythm
Of a hymn he wore close to the book

REMBRADTS PLEIN

Joyous and confused in the safety
Of the café's parameters that square
Upon that one glance glare
Upon the neighbouring tables condiments
As she hid behind that modernist menu

     Eloquently simple how her petticoat
     Combed the pathed coble stones
     Thin tram inclusion

Bank dispursed change as baguettes
Split for French butter; beggars wait
For the squares sparrows as lost squirrels

     Bar kiosk neatly offers nuts with
     Beer that's free as olives in Falafel

Waitress still seem to dance with
Implants, music and meal
Far cry from the factory's
Conveyor belt of Britain
Its all just waiting for shutters
to cover those vibrant stars

     Tucking them to bed with
     Cardboard boxes and Tarpaulin
     By Museum Street off Rokin

CONTENTS

ALL WOMAN   5
THR TONGUE OF FIRE   6
IKEA WOMAN   7
PIE MOCHA   8
COPITO DE NEIUVE (SNOWFLAKE)   9
BLOKES   10
WHY ARE YOU FIXING ON FEELINGS?   11
INTERVIEWING THE CLEANER   12
BEDTIME   14
TRAP DOOR   15
BULLET POINTS   16
PAPER HAIR   17
BOX OF SECRETS   19
THANKS FOR THAT DISSEMINATION   20
Rob B window this is your life   21
NAILED TO A COMPARISON OF COMPATIBILITY   22
FAIRY BIOPSY   24
DRINK UP DRUNK   26
FORGETFUL (NESS)   27
FORGOTTEN (CELL)   28
THINGS GOIN'ON   29
CHAIKUS – PLASTIC BOTTOM   30
SWISH AND SWASH OF WAGES DAY   31
DISTANCE YOURSELF FROM THE BATTLE   32
WOE BETIDE: THE WRECKAGE   33
INVARIABLE FURIOUS ANGER   34
ENVYISM   36
ENVY   37
PERMIT ME TO INTRODUCE MY PRIDE   38
A WORTH WHILE RITUAL   39
WHITE FRILLS   41
THE GENRE NOTION   42
CONCERTINAED POPPIES   44

BIKE SHED   45
LINTEL EYES   46
MANX BUTCHER   47
HYPOCRISY   48
REMBRANDTS PLEIN   49

Published in the United Kingdom by
Br@ndBook London Publishing

e-mail: bookshop@brandbook.co.uk
www.brandbook.co.uk

CONTEMPORARY POETRY SERIES BY
Br@ndBook London Publishing

Józef BARAN	HYMN PORANNY
Józef BARAN	LEARNING FROM AN ANT
Francesco BERNARDINI	LIBERUM VETO
Rob BRIDGE	A MIRRORED WOMEN
Elżbieta WOJNAROWSKA	EROTYKI
Adam ZIEMIANIN	DZIKIE ZAPAŁKI